T0278803

Blue
Yodel

Books by Eleanor Stanford

The Book of Sleep
Bartram's Garden
The Imaginal Marriage
Blue Yodel

Blue Yodel

Eleanor Stanford

Carnegie Mellon University Press
Pittsburgh 2024

Acknowledgments

Thanks to the editors of the following journals, where these poems first appeared:

Bennington Review: "beloved, you said come to me," "How I thought about my body (Driving north through rain)," and "*Where did the handsome beloved go, Rumi, please tell me where*"

The Common: "*a kind of privileged existence that sets it apart from other worlds*," "Lover, before the pandemic (I understood power)," and "Lover, before the pandemic (I bought a pair of suede boots)"

Copper Nickel: "*If we want the benefits of possible worlds, we have to pay for them*" and "Blue Yodel No. 12"

Drunken Boat: "The Lover's House"

The Iowa Review: "*world of objects that are not actual but only could have been*"

Los Angeles Review of Books: "*a lapse of compositional control*" and "*all worlds and all of their denizens are equally real*"

Narrative Magazine: "Talking about History with You (*Hispañola*)"

Poetry Magazine: "beloved, I was driving down"

Poetry Northwest: "*And I, a person not glowing with the strength of strong lions*"

Prairie Schooner: "Vanitas," "Blue Yodel No. 1," and "beloved, thin as smoke and"

The Seneca Review: "I was really getting into my tragic heroine persona"

Zócalo Public Square: "We Were Born"

Thank you to my dear friends for the accompaniment. Thank you to my family for the music. Thank you to Jerry, Cynthia, and Connie at Carnegie Mellon University Press, and to the National Endowment for the Arts and Faberllull Olot for supporting my work.

Book design by So Young Park

Library of Congress Control Number 2024939012
ISBN 978-0-88748-705-7

10 9 8 7 6 5 4 3 2 1

Contents

How I Thought about My Body

A Fake Book

Talking about History with You
Hispañola

A monocausal theory can't be right,
you said. The terrace looked out to the sea.
The blue undimmed, cloud scarred, finite.

You gave me a shard of your past each night.
The stars in Peshawar. A sharp-fisted lychee.
A monocausal theory can't be right.

It rained. The sun came out, too hot, too bright.
You mixed a drink of sugar, rum, brackish debris.
The ice, unlike our thirst, was finite.

Your glowing cigarette outlined our fight.
I'd left my kids behind. Did that mean I was free?
A monocausal theory can't be right.

We burned like that—a flame tree set alight.
In truth, my kids, almost grown, left me.
The past, unlike love's flaws, is finite.

The island burnished its own cruel history.
We slept with windows open. You entered me.
A monocausal theory can't be right.
The past, despite our gloss, is finite.

Bluesette

Leda with her long neck
under the acacias, bent
over the guitar. Below us
on the field
the beautiful boys
arching the ball
into the net. Her fingers
fumble the strings
but her voice refracts
the twilight, cuts
like the broken
bottles along the wall.
How she calls for a glass
of water; scolds the maid,
then kisses her on the cheek.

Flamenco Sketches

Over me
in bed, he slapped
my face—once, twice—
sting of salt
on his palm

In the reeds
the grackles
flashed their red
epaulets,
scattering—

Driving west
on the Atlantic City
Expressway the sun
won't stop
setting—

After all the words
have been emptied—
paved over, burned, sold
at a loss—new words
will grow
there—bitterweed,
switchgrass, stinging nettle

Although as Leibniz
says, even followers
of Copernicus still talk
about the sun
going down

Leibniz also says of memory
if you could become
the King of China but
forgot everything
before—who
would want that?

Miles of highway,
thistle and sharp
stones, the tiny weeds
of death

If I could forget you,
then, beloved, flash of gray
at your temple, salt-
peter rose dissolving—

All Blues

No hell like your nine-year-old
practicing the trumpet.
Early dusk, lathed and lonely
in the gloaming of your devices.
No hell like when your lover's
left for Montreal. It's hardly
another country, he says, ignoring
the ice and laws'
intransigence.
And your children:
their gaze darkened as if
by bruising. How you long
for a color intermediate
between hurt and burning,
for any smutty little touch.

a lapse of compositional control

I liked to hear about my husband's girlfriends: the one who was kidnapped at gunpoint in Niger. The one with a tattoo across her back: of lines, he said, but I heard *lions*, pictured a savannah rippling on skin.

Marriage, like the music of Villa-Lobos, relies on chance procedures, on indeterminacy—*in which performers are given latitude, within certain limits.*

The one who did energy work on his chakras. The one who came to our house when I was away and drank our whiskey, left soggy pad Thai in the fridge.

I want to say that my sentences emerge from the city's skyline, or from imperfections in the paper—the generator of randomness still humming after the lights have gone out.

Bishop to Lowell, on his using an ex-wife's letters in his poems: *art just isn't worth that much.*

Still, if I could have lain down on marriage's grassy plain and let myself be torn limb from limb, devoured—I like to think I would have.

Mas que nada

What river brown
as tea what horse
grazing at the edge
of town what rock-
carved basin deep
and shining what
moon what drowning
boy my husband
pulled from the
glassy cold
what samba
drum what cobbled
moon what cold

Wave

The dark takes me
in its arms,
spins me around
the living room.
The boys
are playing
Jobim as though
Jobim were a
knock-knock joke,
or an elaborate
fourth-grade
word problem. As though
my glass weren't
a lipstick-smudged
mirror, an astringent
kiss, emptying.
The thing
is to find the lull
and allow yourself
to be pulled
under. To ignore the tug
of the subjunctive
in your chest,
the crumbs scattered
on the rug.
As though Jobim
were a two-bit
swell
beckoning—marimba,
cowboy boots,
mother-
of-pearl.

Blue in Green

You won't, you said,
convince me
jealousy's
a virtue.
I was driving
the sinewy spine
of the island,
my eyes on the narrow
road. Banana plants
and jungly debris.
Not even a little?
Last year's hurricane
still a blue-green
contusion
on the mountain's
rib. Not even a little.
But I liked
to think of you
young and sad, supple
as a sapling.
The briny shallows
of your mouth
on another mouth
not mine. Or the quickening
when I watched you
flirt with the Moroccan
bartender in San Juan
who shared
your name. The way a little
acid brightens
the lettuce leaves, or
the muddy creek

stirs with algae
bloom, or how later
I'd savor
the metallic tang
of your armpit.

Vanitas

When I was a young woman, I didn't understand
that my lack of vanity was of no
consequence. Now on the edge
of fifty, I kneel before
my asters and dahlias in an evening
gown. I feed them ground-up
stars, bonemeal. In the apartment
below mine, my ex-husband
and his young bride recline on
a silk-slung divan from Ikea.
Youth with its infinite power lays down
an ultimatum. After a few days in a vase,
the petals descend in a show of surrender
on the kitchen counter. The stems slick
and decadent, sweet stench of rot.
When I was a young woman,
I scorned practice in favor of
feeling. Now I cup the flare
of my iliac crest, unmoved by
lovers' praise. In their frost-draped
bed, the stars of the devil
and clair de lune stare down
the coming cold, feast on the skeletons
of dead sea creatures.

One-Note Samba

E voltei pra minha nota como eu volto pra você

Blue
countable and
uncountable.
Polyphonic blue
of the mango leaves.
Your absence
from my days
that smooth shadow
in the branches,
gleam in dark
water,
that altered note.

Blue Yodel

Evening Song
after Sylvia Plath

We ate overpriced burgers on a patio by the sea.
The light off the water, church bells
echoing from Condado.

On the rocks below, girls in skimpy suits
and glued-on lashes struck lewd poses for TikTok.
I bit into the burger's pink heart.

The sand was strewn with dying seaweed, air
with the call of gulls. A mother is an idea
that gives rise to other ideas.

You looked out, lost in thought, lips
moving silently, reciting the lyrics
to a song. Once I watched you move

across the arc of my belly,
fetal horse galloping through an amniotic dream.
To let you go, I had to drown that young woman.

I held her under until breath stilled, and in her place
the crone rose, laughing, in a dress of tattered algae,
regrets phosphorescing on her skin in the last light.

Blue Yodel No. 1

The beloved leaves for Montreal. Brief Edenic
summer. Briefer fall. The beloved won't turn on
the light, his face thinning into shadow. Sadness
eating holes in the cuffs of his sweater. Says maybe
he'll become a monk, but one who still
sleeps with you sometimes. He wants you
to take other lovers. The beloved says he'll write you
an essay on the mind-body problem. Says he doesn't
get jealous. The beloved puts on
red lipstick silver earrings goes drinking
at Vices & Versa with Silvano or Maya, gets manicures
with Claire. Lover, you are not allowed
to be jealous either. Instead comb the knots from your wet hair.
Strain spaghetti for the children, drink a single whisky
at the El Bar, close your eyes when the band plays "Together
Again."   The beloved doesn't believe
in language anymore   aspires to be a star cactus
            or the snow-dusted habit
of the Carmelite shoveling after a storm.
The beloved says he used to write long love letters but
no long love letters for you, lover. Instead blank sheets,
an empty bed. Your ten-year-old waltzing you
around the living room while his older brother
plays "Goodnight Irene" on the piano.
                    Once the beloved called you
dearest. Once, in a rainforest, knelt and begged
to make you come while a cloud floated across the mountain.
            You need to follow better, your ten-year-old says.

Blue Yodel No. 2

It is good to be tragic. Good
to drink a Citywide
in the Tattooed Mom,
the beloved's absence
an ache predictable as
the Xmas lights behind
the bar, while M. talks
about driving to Queens
to kiss a dulcimer player
who it turned out
had a girlfriend he'd invited
to the gig. Good
to go a drag show with R.,
who has no patience
for the beloved's reticence
and arcane research into
seventeenth-century
Aristotelianism. The singer, in stiletto
boots and a skimpy Santa
dress, does a rendition
of "You Can't Always Get
What You Want" that almost
makes you cry, lover. You
and the entire audience
of senior citizens. It is easy
to feel like a good wife: wash
the dishes do the laundry
make the dinner. Easy to pretend
this life is lucky or calamitous.
What is your life even like,
texts the tattooed millennial
from North Philly you used

to sleep with from time
to time. Don't text
at the dinner table, your child
chastises. K. texts, I could never
be with a bisexual, he'll always
want something you can't
give him. But the beloved
wants many things
you can't give him—the answer
to the mind-body problem,
a houseplant that won't
die, for you to move
to Montreal. Lover, even though
your husband still sometimes
touches the tuning peg
of your hip, even though
your sons tell you
you are beautiful, you'd be lying
if you said it was enough.

Blue Yodel No. 6

The beloved is eating okra
and bitter gourd with his hands
in the city of his childhood. If
language is a skin, you want
to lick the oil-slick conjunctions
from his fingers. Lover,
in your country, there is a rise
in despair tied to the rise
in sea levels and the alt-
right. But you, lover, prefer
your despair timeless
and apolitical. Prefer Penelope
with her skein and many
suitors. Or pedal steel
and a voice like cracked
china in the bar,
someone not
the beloved leaning in
to touch your cheek.
The beloved is still
asleep, or waking
from a dream
of trains to tea
and the finches singing
in the kitchen. Later, in bed,
someone not the beloved will
undress you, touch the leafstalk
of your shoulder. Lover,
you have no skin. When you ask
why he didn't text he will say,
awed at the beauty
of his indifference: I didn't
think of you at all.

beloved, I was driving down

Girard   the trolley tracks'
steel harmonics   humming
it was dark and
in a poorly heated room
north of Pine a lover waited to
dismantle me   Yoyo Ma was
playing the cello suites
again   they echoed in the
ribcages of the
squats on 54th my thighs
lace-encased   glissando of
black stockings   the suites
begin with what the instrument
can do   cunning hook
and eye of the garter belt
progress to   what it cannot
beloved in the piebald
park between the cemetery and
the dollar store the monkey bars
sang with cold   Bach makes us
hold one note in mind so
we can hear several as though
at once   here on Eid you held
my hand   other people's
families converged and
the   dark tremolo of
goat smoke rose   sweat pressed
the sundress to the small of
my back   beloved I listened
to you wishing your mother
on the phone   a sweet breaking
of the fast   it's a trick of the

baroque beloved   those old
notes the mind keeps trying
to hold onto   before I left
the house my son who is almost
seventeen   played me a song
he wrote called
"Doctor Misery"   *your baby*
left you   he sang   beloved
in the illuminated laundromat
on 47th the clothes rotated
to the cello's churn   to a
police siren's wolf tone   my own
body was once
so pure only one person
touched it and only
on Fridays so pure it spun
water and fiber into gold
music Ma says   is not one
thing   look beloved
inside my uterus a gear-
box inside the ridges
of my sex a mountain
range   beloved, when
you left it was another
December   you folded
your many colored
scarves   sealed your
books into boxes now
in a blank room in another
city you are writing an
academic paper on
perfection you chop

carrots into bright coins
dusk's adagio on snow outside
you touch the dancer's hip
point   lift that long
bowed note from her
mouth   you told me
beloved there are two
kinds of perfection: order
and seeing things as they
are   the cello constructs
a galaxy of neutron
stars from the flicker of
light in each row house
on Resurrection Blvd
the well-ordered scene in the
crumbling Victorian where
my lover slides a hand under
my skirt undoes my
bindings   in the body
cavity   it is the emptiness
that makes air
reverberate it is the
emptiness that sings

Blue Yodel No. 9

Mexico City, the pulquería dark
and noisy at four in the afternoon,
fermented sap of the maguey cactus
in plastic pitchers, the beloved's hand
on your thigh. But no, that must have
been the year before, on the cracked
stoop in Kingsessing or the veranda
in the rainforest, an island you pretended
was another country, when the beloved
reached for you like that.
But you, lover, were still hopelessly
in love's thrall, following his long
easy strides through the pullulating
streets, the horns and swerving
taxis, innards sizzling on food carts,
the endless particulars
unfolding, as though
one metropolis were the same
as another—Bangkok, Mexico City,
Karachi—sweat burnished, neon
buzzing. On the balcony
in the evening you watched the lightning over
the mountains, smoking the loosies
the beloved pulled carefully from
his pocket, having bought them
from a street vendor, one of his
small, exact pleasures: pink polish
on his clean nails, old Dylan songs
while you played Scrabble.
The blue yodel, Dylan says,
defies the rational
and conjecturing mind. So too,

the beloved. The gravity
of his spare form, each of his silences
an entire city, knife sharpeners
pedaling their whetstones
through narrow streets.

Blue Yodel No. 12

Your anarchist is too sad for sex.
His mother is dying of cancer
and his lesbian girlfriend about
to leave him. Sometimes her profile
appears on your dating apps. Sometimes
you read the books on her bedside
table while your anarchist showers:
identity politics and critical theory
from the eighties. You are trying
to think of how to say this
in a poem: he is very good
at going down on you.
You are sorry about his mother
and his girlfriend, but also a little bit
indignant. You spend a long time
staring at a sentence
in one of his girlfriend's
books, a quote from Anaïs Nin
about how women's art should
bleed or nourish like a womb or leak
milk. A more accurate way to say it
is no one has ever been this good
at going down on anyone else
in the history of the world. His aptitude
is ahistorical,
implausible as the haunches
of megafauna or the enduring
appeal of poststructural ideology. Even if
his idea of a date is walking
four blocks in the February wind
to put his friend's trash
on the curb. Perhaps this

is the tenderness you feel
driving home in the early
morning, pale sunrise through
the power lines of West Philly—
it is the tenderness of one
ice age for another.

Improved by Fire

Dominoes

We were playing dominoes in my friend's back-
yard on Baring Street. I had reached the end
of my marriage: a cloud-numb June. He built a fire
out of a dismantled piano.
The air was the same as my body.
I shuffled the tiles, which are also called men.

In the last years, there had been a number of men.
A dentist, two philosophers, an anarchist with a bad back.
An engineer worried about the mind-body
problem. Dominoes is a game of ends—
of reassembling bones into arms and trees. The piano
reassembled itself as smoke. A piano on fire

has been called The End of Civilization. Fire
is one way to be consumed. Another is men.
I decided to keep playing until the piano
stopped making sounds, said the artist. His back
was turned to the setting sun. The end
of my marriage was like that: the body

of the artist pitted against the piano's body.
It didn't matter. The fire
would win in the end.
The man on Baring Street blurred into other men.
The piano must be one no builder could bring back.
It should be an upright, the irretrievable piano.

It wasn't fair to my friend. Who asks the piano
how it wants to leave its body?
I tried to bring myself back—
moon on the painted ferns, fire

on the face of the tiles, my men
lined up. My friend's hand brushing the ends

of my hair. I laid a blank at the open end.
On another dark street, my sons at the piano.
From childhood's lit spinet, they emerge as men,
brush off the embers. Once my body
was such an instrument of fire.
But the keys are gone. I can't get them back.

After reckoning the score, we lay on our backs
on a lawn chair. His hands on my body
soft as piano-ash, small endnote of fire.

beloved, thin as smoke and

glamorous you slipped into
the scrubland of
my feral hair
beloved I built you from
black bile and Dylan lyrics
from skeins of
gossip about end-
times and the Humean non-
self beloved I sent you
by mail a tin of
sugared ginger a silk
thong I masturbated in
beloved I gave you
a childhood in
a far-off city by the
sea a feminine soul
beloved have you
noticed that all the seasons
happen at once now
the cherry blossoms
going bananas in
November my own
girlhood catching
fire again and again I
gave you the dropped
stitch of early trauma
and a nervous breakdown
at twenty-three when
you saw God gave you Ceres for
a mother moping in her sky-
blue sari for your June
return I built you

to make me kneel and
take you in my mouth
beloved after days
of silence I said
I miss you I remembered you
rolling weed and
tobacco talking about
the Critique of Pure
Reason your elegant
fingers your brilliant
legerdemain my shoes
wet from the muddy
field where I kept
waiting for flame

beloved, you said come to me

wanting neither to
possess nor be   possessed
I was in the bath   reading
about strategic nonviolent
conflict   a lover
texted me a hotel room
scene   I knelt on a
bed kissing another
woman   moaning while
he took turns
eating us out   my feet
made smudged blossoms
in the grime of the tub
What if the results were
undeniable—
a child called
mom get out can I
have the bath now—*but the*
loyalists refused
to accept them   I dried my
heat-flushed skin   began walking
north   through New
Jersey   the wilds of
strip malls   my wet
hair froze into gnarled
branches   I remembered
it was already another
century   thank god
I climbed aboard a
Megabus dozed with my
cheek on the cold
window through post-

apocalyptic Times
Square even in that other
century I had remembered
to text you good morning
and good night and *I waited*
a long time—Master—but
I can wait more remembered
the building at 48th and Market
that once proclaimed in spray
paint For What I Want
I Can Wait   I Can Wait 4800 Years
If I Have To but last time
I drove past it had been
torn down   you hated when
I called you Master
when I became Simone
de Beauvoir sobbing for
Sartre on the cobbled
streets of Douarnenez
a storm brewing off
the coast of France beloved
would I have possessed
you when I was   twenty-three
I was still chubby
then   would you have
licked the salt that gathered
in pressed bouquets in my
armpits and at the back of
my neck I watched some other
state unfold itself
stubbled fields shifting
sky of starlings   inside

my phone   the children
wanting dinner   lovers wanting
dirty pics and to laugh
at my antic life my mother
asking *did you just*
call me? my phone won't
ring   beloved would you
have possessed me
then your long hair to your
hips your shy dark
fire sly tongue
come to me wanting
neither   you said and then it was
snowing   then the trees and
the trees etc. you hate it
when I genuflect when I
beg   Dora Maar in a white
swimsuit   Dora Maar in
the studio   photographing
Guernica   who wrote
I wasn't Picasso's
mistress   he was
just my master
neither possessing nor
possessed   when I
was twenty-three I held
sadness in a tin cup
poured it over my naked
shoulders   in a village
no one has ever
heard of   even the people
who live there can't agree

if it exists or not
Dora Maar who enchanted
her master with her pale blue
eyes and her masochism
Dora Maar   who wrote
after Picasso   God
I crossed the
border on foot up-
state somewhere in
the woods   kept
walking

world of objects that are not actual
but only could have been

Your mother keeps finches in her kitchen in Karachi. She shows
me the size with her hand: small distance between thumb and
forefinger. All afternoon, she cooked eggplant and okra that we
eat mostly in silence. In her food, the vestiges of your childhood:
bitter seeds. Spokes of a collapsed star. *Oh, already grown*, she says,
when I tell her the ages of my sons: nine, twelve, fourteen. *Soon they
will fly away,* she says. No vestiges in this world of the dark-eyed
grandchildren, her fingers pinching their delicious cheeks. In this
world, no vestiges either of those altricial bodies that once looked up
at me, open-mouthed, translucent with need. Later you walk me out
in the rain, push me up against the car, kiss me hard. No vestiges
of the stars' sharp beaks, or the neighborhood children's feathered
chalk on the sidewalk.

The Lover's House

The lover's house is improved by fire.
—Rumi

I waited for you in Barcelona.

I waited for you in Prague.

I waited for you in the dentist's chair: head thrown back, mouth wide open, unable to speak.

I waited for you on the bus north, listening to Rihanna, watching the olive trees wring their hands.

I waited for you on a bridge in the rain.

I waited for you in the car, driving my twelve-year-old to his piano lesson, talking about math homework and the end of the world.

I waited for you at the end of the world.

I waited for you in red gingham, in a sepia photograph, an unreadable look in my eyes.

I waited for you in a church.

I waited for you in a stone forest, in a tree's vestibule.

I tried calling you on stolen Wi-Fi from the Kentucky Fried Chicken across from the Sagrada Familia.

I waited for you in the movie theater till the final credits. In the ancient amphitheater, all the actors moving without sound.

In the bowl of blueberries, I waited: the last sour green knot.

I waited for you in my bed, where I read a 600-page history of debt, and also several self-help books about love, where I ate frozen yogurt popsicles and watched a show in which Nicole Kidman plays a creepy New Age Russian guru.

I waited for you in another century. Sometimes as a woman, sometimes a man.

I waited for you in someone else's bed.

I waited for you in the Wegman's between the rainbow chard and the cheese counter.

I tried calling you from the closet of my parents' house during Thanksgiving dinner.

I waited in the smoke from the fire pit.

I waited without a coat in January.

The next time I tried calling it was Passover, I was in the bathroom, half-drunk, while we were still wandering in the desert, eating bitter herbs and making fun of the script we were supposed to be following.

I waited for you instead of "setting an intention" or "extending my side body" or "raising my hands to my third-eye center."

I waited for you on the banks of my marriage, staring into the murky shallows.

I waited for you in the soft blade of your fern, the shined spathe of your anthurium.

I waited in the locked chest of your childhood, with the wedding and funeral saris, smelling of bitter camphor.

When the Berlin Wall fell, when the ice caps started invisibly melting, I had already been waiting for you a long time.

I waited for you on the corner of 47th and Baltimore.

When I thought I had been waiting for a long time, I thought about the Sagrada Familia, which has been under construction continuously since 1882.

I waited for you on the dating apps, waited for your face to appear behind the next software engineer or financial analyst posing in front of the Eiffel Tower.

In English, it is possible to wait without hope.

I waited for you in a market stall in Karachi, in the names of the fruits you touched and weighed and cradled.

I waited for you in the airport.

Every time a plane touched down or lifted off, I wanted to text you.

I waited for you when my fifteen-year old son told me he would never respect me again for as long as I live.

I waited for you when I didn't know if I was supposed to laugh or cry.

I waited to call you, and once or twice I didn't.

I waited for you the way I waited for my period.

I waited for you the ways Jews wait for the Mashiach.

I tried to tell myself that the waiting meant I was in touch with the cycles of suffering and rebirth, that I should be grateful.

I was waiting for you when the factories and schools shut down and the airplanes stopped flying.

When sea lions lounged on the sidewalks of Buenos Aires and the smog lifted over Beijing and Mumbai, I waited for you.

I waited for you all summer, from the first incandescent magnolia blossom to the last yellow leaves.

I waited for you in New Jersey, while the waters rose along Atlantic Avenue.

I waited for you in the pine barrens, where there was no cell service.

I waited for you in the future that had already happened.

I waited for you in the future that would never happen.

I waited for you by getting stoned and submerging myself in water so hot the entire bathroom disappeared.

I waited for you under the tree of awe.

I waited for you on the fire escape in late April, the sun going down and my shoulders pinned to the sky.

Lover, before the pandemic

I understood power
as the ability to excite
desire. When I passed
the socialists camped out
in the square in Mexico City
last summer I cringed
in recognition and took a picture
that I texted to my anarchist
in another country. Later
I bought silver earrings
in the market in Coyoacán.
On the Airbnb's creaky bed
with you, I conjured
Frida and Diego's vivid
fits of jealousy.
Do you not possess,
lover, like political systems,
a strong, articulated
discourse? You do not.
Once, not long ago,
I was a city
laid low by desire.
Now I'm an empire
of indifference,
tending the borders
of my pallid daffodils.

Dispatches

I called you from the kitchen in Charlottesville, holding a baby
on one hip and scrubbing a cast iron pan. You were in floating in
the sea off Zanzibar. I called you from a black volcanic hillside in
the middle of the Atlantic Ocean. You were in a refugee camp in
Kenya, listening to stories about war. The baby was a translucent
ghost on the ultrasound machine. You asked me what to make
for dinner. Rice and beans, I said. I called you from the island in
the Atlantic where I was pounding dried maize. There were no
phone lines. Chicken noodle soup, I said. I called you in Jerusalem.
You were wearing a sundress, trying to understand the history of
conflict. You were hours before me. You were hours behind. We
were taking our temperatures. We were trying to get pregnant.
The baby was learning to drive. The baby got her period and had
a crush on Shawn Mendes. We were trying not to get pregnant.
You sent me a ginger root thick as a fist from the San Fernando
Valley. The doctor in Nairobi told you to pray to Jesus. Foccacia,
you said. Chickpea ratatouille. I sent you Joni Mitchell longing for
California. You sent me a fertility sculpture from Addis Ababa, its
carved wooden form the blessing and curse we tied to our backs all
those years.

Lover, before the pandemic

I bought a pair
of suede boots
on Rue St. Laurent.
I knelt supplicant
before you, begged you
to hit me harder
then smoked a joint
on your balcony, went over
fine points of Aristotle.
The cross on the mountain
rusted. You are
insane, you text now
from your country
that's closed its borders
to my own. But lover,
I am the soldier
of nothing. Not blowjobs
or boutiques,
not bitterness
or social distancing.
Lover, I can recall
only two things I imparted
to my sixteen-year-old
this year: the meaning
of no atheists
in a foxhole, and that in sex
pleasing the woman
is what matters. Now
I lie down
in the cold rain and shiver,
wait for the chard to germinate
and the medical system
to collapse.

Where did the handsome beloved go, Rumi, please tell me where

The anarchist asked me if I believed in God. We were in bed,
and it was snowing. I needed a mirror to make sure I existed.
He touched my rib cage under my shirt and kept talking about
economic forces. You can't let him tear you to shreds, Jess said on
the phone. Rumi thought the handsome beloved might have become
a cypress tree. Were you crying again, the anarchist said. I passed
him the vape pen. I thought the handsome beloved was more likely
a mistranslation, a blossoming sage plant. We were in bed, talking
urgently about Chernobyl. He wanted to tell me about probability.
Do you want to switch roles, I said. The anarchist showed me the
trees his mother looked at as she was dying. He needed someone to
fix the roof. But as soon as I said it I realized that I did not want to
switch roles, that what I needed was to continue to surrender. It was
snowing. The handsome beloved was a repetition compulsion. The
bed was covered in deep snow. More blew in, carrying chokecherry
petals and radiation dust. Sometimes I hated the handsome beloved,
but he was always the beloved. When I left the next afternoon,
the anarchist gave me a menorah and a pair of his dead mother's
hiking sandals.

Lover, in the third month of the pandemic

I order a white flowered bikini
for a trip I won't
take with you.
Matisse, confined to his room
in Villa le Rêve during the war, turned
the memory of the South Pacific
and a bird-shaped stain on the wall
into Oceania, the Sky. Confined
to your apartment
in Montreal, you tell me that whenever
you are on an airplane,
you feel calm. This is
like that, you say. At night,
I sit on the couch
and hold hands with my
son who is almost
eleven and watch small
bright fish move through
the reef's outstretched arms
without touching them. This is
like that, I think. I turn it off
when David Attenborough starts
talking about how all the coral
is dying. I dream of
your mouth lapping at me
like the sea. Sometimes,
lover, in a flash, I wake up
and reverse the direction
of my fall. When asked
how he entered his abstraction
of air and underwater
women, Matisse said,
I became a parakeet.

I was really getting into
my tragic heroine persona,

my Joan Didion in dark glasses, my long-
suffering Loretta Lynn. Getting into
my tragic heroine chic: multi-tiered tulle
gown, black eyeliner, boxing gloves. I flung
myself into the carriage, young son
clinging to my skirt, left Petersburg. In lieu
of my spine, a wheat stalk. In lieu of a worldview,
a bruise. The psychoanalyst's opinion:
the heroine turns tragic when hunger
mutilates her. But first, the heavy-lidded look,
the laudanum. The younger men who flayed
my wounds until I came. Sharp-edged languor,
exquisite abasement. Before the wanting took
its knife to me, I savored the blade.

Lover, before the pandemic

it was summer, and my
anarchist insisted
we watch Love and Death,
though it was well past
the time of watching Woody
Allen ironically, or at all,
so it meant we could hate
both him and ourselves
in the sui generis way of American
Jews. You were a shadow
on the sun I squinted at
across the Atlantic, giving a paper
in Ghent and getting drunk
with Kant scholars. My husband
at home with the kids. Lover, if then
I had no shame
it was because shame
seemed distant and obsolete
as the Pleistocene
but just today I read a story
in the paper about Pablo Escobar's
hippos lounging happy
and forgotten in the Magdalena
River, and the unexpected
providence of rewilding.

How I Thought about My Body

If we want the benefits of possible worlds, we have to pay for them

I am growing a new mother in my kitchen. Primordial, glistening, suspended in a jar of sweet black tea.

Just as cheese is made out of milk: one explanation for how the universe began. *Worms appeared in it, and these were the angels.*

There were years when my only hobbies were growing other people with my body, and fermenting things. Sour milk. Yeast spores. The kitchen counter spinning with possible worlds.

Hildegard of Bingen: *her womb was pierced like a net with many openings, with a huge multitude of people running in and out*

The mother floats in her transparent cage.

Oh, and composting. How tenderly I saved the banana peels, the coffee grounds. With what care I turned the heap, noted the double-leafed cucurbits sprouting from the loamy dark.

She is porous as cheesecloth, the mother. A multitude of people running in and out.

Hildegard: *a woman as large as a great city.*

The new mother gathers herself from the shreds.

How I thought about my body

Viola pomposa. Archlute. End pin.
Bow-ache on strings, its too-bright shimmer.
The soul is echo of external things,
said Leibniz. Crumhorn. Dulcimer.

I slid a shard of soap across my shoulder.
The qualm of clavichord, its baroque fretting
that makes the tone less sweet, but bolder.
To touch its keys compels forgetting.

The voice in the wilderness of your head.
Her vagina was the only vehement
sign of her existence, Clarice said.
The fundamental pitch our ears invent

even when it isn't there. As from afar
you cradle my neck and comb my hair.

all worlds and all of their denizens are equally real

Maria Santana shows me the map she is making of the quilombos: specks of light where the hands of slaves' descendants catch babies. Her own daughter flickers, a small star in a distant interior. How to escape the body? Maria shrugs: a cosmology of cigarette smoke around her shoulders, her field notes annotated with ash.

In 1934, Villa-Lobos insisted: *I create music out of necessity, biological necessity.* His piano an incandescent extension of his hands, or of his mind. What did Villa-Lobos know of biological necessity? From another hemisphere, my sons exert their gravitational tug.

The only way to escape the body is through the body.

When I birthed them, I was bigger than that pain, planetary.

Villa-Lobos released his composition to the will of the stars. But Villa-Lobos was also a shill for the military dictatorship.

How I thought about my body

The sun glinting off the salt fields. An island
where I lived when I was young. Self-reliant
fallacy. The coast eroding. Defiant
child running toward the sea. Guile and

need. Fallacy fallacy. Unplanned
city straining its borders: Crow. Saint
Barbara. Inkwell. Fig Tree. Ancient
extraction tool jutting from the salt pans.

The island dissolved. Or didn't exist.
Its name was Salt. Its roads unpaved.
Its gullies dry. A fallacy of form
and content. Galaxy of dirt and mist.
Its name was Fire, Holy, Brave.
I huddled powerless against its storm.

The Story

The dancer was forty-two and wanted a baby.

In my fantasies, you are with another woman. She is Egyptian and wearing a hijab. She is French Canadian with eyes the color of a frozen lake. In my fantasies, I am watching.

In November, you thought you might die of cold and lack of touch.

I was walking up a hill toward a lighthouse. I was sleepless in the bed of a lover. I was standing before a hedge of twilit hydrangeas.

In my fantasy, you are smoothing the sleeves of your purple kameez with embroidery at the collar. Putting on your silver earrings, singing a song to yourself before she arrives.

I came to see that if I found the story I would find redemption.

The dancer had a story. She was too old to be a dancer and was pondering her next career move.

In my fantasies, you are not telling me you are considering becoming a sperm donor for the dancer.

You had a story, too. I thought it involved inserting a knife behind my sternum. But your story was waking at five, watering the dahlias on the balcony, reading Descartes in Latin.

The knife was incidental to your story.

In my fantasies, you do not say: why would I turn down a chance to do good?

In my fantasies, I do not have to say, Yes, why. I do not hold still and wait.

Midlife: A Minor Mishap

The anarchist and I were writing a self-help book. We kept our notes under the bed with the sex toys.

We ran a bath, but there was no hot water. We built a fire, and the entire house filled with smoke.

We gave each other Maoist critiques. I overcooked the salmon. He had the emotional life of a leopard gecko. I cried and coerced him into sex. He broke the oil pan on the Prius when he was trying to replace it.

We couldn't agree on who to plagiarize. He wanted Buber: *Forty years, and how far along are you?*

We looked for morels in the woods, but the morels were well hidden.

I preferred Barthes: *I am engulfed, I succumb.*

How I thought about my body

You are exquisite, a man who didn't
want me said. He paused to touch my hair.
In Portuguese, the word means strange:
exquisito. Once, in a forest on the edge
of Salvador, I'd plucked a live termite
from a tree and eaten it. Wings' intimate
cellophane, delicate crunch of exoskeleton.
He was a linguist, so must have known
the taste of arrested flight: that in Rome the word
meant *sought out.* On the stern limestone face
of Kentish coast, it meant *precise.* Exquisite,
he said, then added, like a curse: you know that.

Poem by the Bridge at Olot

How long will I grieve the marriage that I ruined?
Every afternoon at four, the fog's soft tongue, fluent
in thin solace. Or worse, the sun comes out.
I take a bath and wait for dinner.
Each vowel's a city, says Catalan for beginners.
Emilio the waiter brings red wine and wild boar.
It's not like I've escaped a war.

At the Museum of Saints, we watch the careful surgeons
amputate. Drawers labeled Crowns of Thorns, Small Virgins.
If someone says it's art, it's art, the abstract painter
says. Hiking up the mountain, we stop to fill our gourd
with holy water. I'm too hung up on being good.
Collecting evidence and ex-votos of divorce.
Less concerned with theory or aesthetic wars.

The photographer creates illusions in the landscape.
Uses mirrors to make half my body a driftwood scrap.
I'm a bleak vista in her telephoto lens.
Maybe art's a disappearing act.
Can you replace my thoughts with a briar patch
of stars? I ask. In the field, a crop of doors.
In the framing lies the art of war.

You can't outsmart your melancholy or your dead.
Tell us what you hate about your life, the Syrian said.
Easy. I hate that I'm American, tone-deaf and too sensitive.
He's bitter, funny and depressive
but faithful to his Danish wife.
What writer's not an opportunist? My luck this self-inflicted scar.
His the looping echo of the war.

People still live in these walled cities,
drive their fancy cars down crooked stone eternities.
At the gift shop, I buy a postcard I won't send.
Dear N., I write, on the back of a medieval oubliette.
Then hold the corner to a match, light a hand-rolled cigarette.
Truth's less convincing than metaphor.
The ancients knew that when they went to war.

a kind of privileged existence that sets it apart from other worlds

All summer, I sit on the porch, my son appearing, disappearing. Walls of rain or night, of larkspur, bleeding heart. The stone floor long ago lifted from the lion's den.

Translator's note: Having children is a way of remaking oneself.

Somewhere between sunset and bed, between fireflies' ellipses and his desperate texting, I beg him to play the saddest songs on his father's guitar. "Swinging Doors." "Will the Circle Be Unbroken."

Translator's note: The wish is to conjoin remnants of some illusory self with a new undiluted self against the disintegrations of time.

If I hum a few bars, his fingers find the chords. *How do you know?* I ask. My son shrugs, his face bioluminescent. *I don't*, he says. *I listen.*

We Were Born
for Ezra

We were born
on the same day.
Under a full moon,
in a cold snap.
Through a series
of continental collisions
at the headwaters
of the Rivanna River.
The doctor said
get out of the bathtub.
We were born in a bed
with stirrups. In a room
with bright lights. We were born
before we knew better.
The doctor said push.
We were born: passengers
on a boat, brimming
glasses on a tray, sweet and sour
spheres on a passionflower vine.
We were born under the same
sign. Mirror-dark, thrown back
by a body or a surface
of light. The doctor said do you want
this baby to be born today
or tomorrow. We said
today. We were born
at the same minute:
11:55 p.m., in a city
entirely independent of any
county, in the autonomous region
east of the oldest mountains
in the world.

How I thought about my body

Driving north through rain, I watched the Schuylkill
outgrow its banks. I'd packed three dildos,
an eighth of weed, a Danish novel:
the coffin that is childhood, the shadows

of old longing at the end. And in between,
streetlights and moon, loneliness, methadone,
a stolen jar of marmalade. I mean,
I thought about the edges: backbone,

burning nerves, closed borders. I wanted
to escape, but also be contained. We
built a fire, drank some wine. The blunted
smolder of damp wood, a stark tableau of trees.

We talked about the history of glass.
Outside, the forest, fog, and meadow grass.

Game Theory

Games are sandwiched between pastimes and intimacy.
—Eric Berne

You played striker on Tuesday nights. On Wednesdays, you showed me your bruises.

I played Wounded in Love, the Tragic Heroine, once in awhile, unconvincingly, Artemis with her Bow and Arrow.

We never played Frigid Woman or Sweetheart.

The rules were clear but unspoken.

I made the bed in the morning. You prepared the coffee.

You could sleep with other people when I wasn't around. I could sleep with other people if I narrated it to you later.

Once in awhile you broke the rules to show me you could.

You egged me on to play The Stocking Game. Bought a tangle of secondhand lingerie on eBay and told me to pose.

With your friends, you played pickle ball and soccer tennis and a long board game rehashing the Spanish Civil War.

You never invited me to game night.

You played Wooden Leg. Also known as Bad Back, or Leaky Roof. The thesis of Wooden Leg is, "What do you expect of a man with a wooden leg?"

You played Schlemiel.
I had no choice but to play Schlemazel.

At our last breakfast on your mom's patio in the country, you handed me a bowl of blackberries and told me you wanted to play the field.

Sometimes it felt like you were playing God, creating me from the bacterial substrate of your mouth.

Our games were sandwiched between your statistical methods and my melancholy spells. Between your mother dying and my divorce.

I brought you zinnias from my garden. You brought me a yellow sundress you found in a trash pile.

I wanted to believe the game we were playing was an infinitely long one. But we both knew it was discrete and continuous.

Twenty years ago, when you were seventeen, your older sister lit a match and intentionally burned your childhood home to the ground.

Driving to your house in West Philly, I played George Jones in the car and sang along, loud and sappy. *I've burnt all my bridges, and I've sunk all my ships.*

If I felt something smoldering in my chest, I reminded myself that a pile of dry leaves can burst into self-generated flames.

I was trying to play you for time.

Want Out is only played by inmates who do not actually want to get out.

You were trying to play me for time, too.
At the creek that last evening, the August light flickered

contrapuntal on the leaves and we watched two golden retrievers splash and tussle.

Once or twice I played If It Weren't For You.

Once in awhile you played Look How Hard I Tried.

New World

In the New World, it's spring.

In the New World, it's raining and you're almost divorced and on the bus to New York to meet a guy from an app, the one Rebecca called the Delectable Desi Dentist.

In the Old World, a battle is raging through the pine forests and gently rolling hills of Luhansk.

In the Old World, you washed cloth diapers and hung them up to dry. You thought nothing, in the Old World, of naming a newborn for a prophet.

In the New World, horses roamed the grasslands. Chicago and Des Moines waited below the soil to bloom.

In the Old World, you said the old words.

In the Old World, you wore lipstick and cried in a tiny wrought-iron elevator.

In the New World, you put on different costumes, scraps of lace, complicated straps.

In the New World, our bodies are controlled by the state.

In the Old World, too.

In the Old World, children harvesting cobalt atop slag heaps.

In the New World, iPhones.

Horses grazing in the New World on the New Jersey Turnpike, a rill, a stand of marsh grass, a rotting tire.

In the Old World, silks and debt.

In the New World, you let the dentist pay for dinner, kiss you in the bar, take you back to his apartment in Cobble Hill.

In the New World, Seven Cities of Gold. All the cafes in Brooklyn overflowing for brunch.

In the New World, the grief of new green and no dam to stem the rising river.

And I, a person not glowing with the strength of strong lions

My friend is building a pyre on which to hang her wedding dress, her children's baby clothes.

Plath, in her letters: *I rode my bike to a fire.*

Years ago, this friend and I used to take our children to the zoo and stare at the mother minding her pride behind the glass.

Now we are nailing planks together. Gathering kindling, erecting a cage of small sticks.

Impossible world of the past, burning.

In bed you read to me from the glowing screen. Something about Kant and teleology. Your voice the timber of a ship, extending up from the keel.

Humans were meant to discover fire, my son told me yesterday. He was collecting stones for a fire pit. Lining them up in a circle.

You'd applied for a postdoc in Kazakhstan. *Maybe I'll learn to ride a horse, you said.*

Muscular sparks catching in a gust, galloping across that grassy possible world.

Hildegard of Bingen called herself a rib. Said *fragile* but meant—I want to think—bewilderment.

And this world, its strong legs, skirt flapping in the wind, heading toward flame.

Previous titles in the Carnegie Mellon Poetry Series

2014

Night Bus to the Afterlife, Peter Cooley
Alexandria, Jasmine Bailey
Dear Gravity, Gregory Djanikian
Pretenders, Jeff Friedman
How I Went Red, Maggie Glover
All That Might Be Done, Samuel Green
Man, Ricardo Pau-Llosa
The Wingless, Cecilia Llompart

2015

The Octopus Game, Nicky Beer
The Voices, Michael Dennis Browne
Domestic Garden, John Hoppenthaler
We Mammals in Hospitable Times, Jynne Dilling Martin
And His Orchestra, Benjamin Paloff
Know Thyself, Joyce Peseroff
cadabra, Dan Rosenberg
The Long Haul, Vern Rutsala
Bartram's Garden, Eleanor Stanford

2016

Something Sinister, Hayan Charara
The Spokes of Venus, Rebecca Morgan Frank
Adult Swim, Heather Hartley
Swastika into Lotus, Richard Katrovas
The Nomenclature of Small Things, Lynn Pedersen
Hundred-Year Wave, Rachel Richardson
Where Are We in This Story, Sarah Rosenblatt
Inside Job, John Skoyles
Suddenly It's Evening: Selected Poems, John Skoyles

2017

Disappeared, Jasmine V. Bailey
Custody of the Eyes, Kimberly Burwick
Dream of the Gone-From City, Barbara Edelman
Sometimes We're All Living in a Foreign Country, Rebecca Morgan Frank
Rowing with Wings, James Harms
Windthrow, K. A. Hays

We Were Once Here, Michael McFee
Kingdom, Joseph Millar
The Histories, Jason Whitmarsh

2018
World Without Finishing, Peter Cooley
May Is an Island, Jonathan Johnson
The End of Spectacle, Virginia Konchan
Big Windows, Lauren Moseley
Bad Harvest, Dzvinia Orlowsky
The Turning, Ricardo Pau-Llosa
Immortal Village, Kathryn Rhett
No Beautiful, Anne Marie Rooney
Last City, Brian Sneeden
Imaginal Marriage, Eleanor Stanford
Black Sea, David Yezzi

2019
The Complaints, W. S. Di Piero
Brightword, Kimberly Burwick
Ordinary Chaos, Kimberly Kruge
Blue Flame, Emily Pettit
Afterswarm, Margot Schilpp

2020
Build Me a Boat: Words for Music 1968–2018, Michael Dennis Browne
Sojourners of the In-Between, Gregory Djanikian
The Marksman, Jeff Friedman
Disturbing the Light, Samuel Green
Any God Will Do, Virginia Konchan
My Second Work, Bridget Lowe
Flourish, Dora Malech
Petition, Joyce Peseroff
Take Nothing, Deborah Pope

2021
The One Certain Thing, Peter Cooley
The Knives We Need, Nava EtShalom
Oh You Robot Saints!, Rebecca Morgan Frank

Dark Harvest: New & Selected Poems, 2001–2020, Joseph Millar
Glorious Veils of Diane, Rainie Oet
Yes and No, John Skoyles

2022
Out Beyond the Land, Kimberly Burwick
All the Hanging Wrenches, Barbara Edelman
Anthropocene Lullaby, K. A. Hays
The Woman with a Cat on Her Shoulder, Richard Katrovas
Bel Canto, Virginia Konchan
There's Something They're Not Telling Us, Kimberly Kruge
A Long Time to Be Gone, Michael McFee
Bassinet, Dan Rosenberg

2023
Night Wing over Metropolitan Area, John Hoppenthaler
Phone Ringing in a Dark House, Rolly Kent
Fleeing Actium, Ricardo Pau-Llosa
Approximate Body, Danielle Pieratti
Wild Liar, Deborah Pope
Joy Ride, Ron Slate
That Other Life, Joyce Sutphen
Sonnets with Two Torches and One Cliff, Robert Thomas

2024
Accounting for the Dark, Peter Cooley
Shine, Joseph Millar
Those Absences Now Closest, Dzvinia Orlowsky
Blue Yodel, Eleanor Stanford
Her Breath on the Window, Karenmaria Subach
Museum of the Soon to Depart, Andy Young